My Vocabulary Notebook
© Christine Draper, 2024

This book was published on the land of the Noongar Whadjuk people. We acknowledge the traditional owners and linguists of this land.

All rights reserved. No part of this book may be reproduced or transmitted in any form or by any means without written permission of the author.

Published: Warru Press, Rockingham 2024
ISBN: 978-1-922819-05-5

How to improve your vocabulary

Vocabulary is important for effective communication because it allows individuals to express their ideas clearly and precisely. It is also important to important to expand your ability to understand new concepts and engage in meaningful conversations across different subjects. It will help you building a strong foundation for reading comprehension and writing skills.
Here are some tips on how you or your child can improve their vocabulary.

- Reading. Reading is the number one method for improving vocabulary. However, it is important that you read a variety of different books, including books that are challenging to read.
- Use a dictionary, physical or online. When you come across an unknown word, don't just skip over it or ignore it but look up the meaning in a dictionary and write it down.
- Make a list of words you don't know. This book is a great place to do this.
- Put the word into a sentence. For example, if I look up the word "ample" I find that it means "enough or more than enough, plentiful." So I might make the sentence "This eleven plus course provides me with ample homework."
- Go back to the root of the word and see how it is made up.
- Play vocabulary games. Games like Scrabble™ or Boggle™ can make learning new words fun.
- Repetition. It has been shown that if we look at something in the short, medium and long term, we are much more likely to remember it. So review your lists.
- Converse with family and friends. Simply talking to people can help improve your vocabulary.
- Use technology. Using Quizlet (quizlet.com) or other quiz and flashcard websites, where you can enter your words and practice them. This can be a really fun way to learn your vocabulary.

How to use this book.

Vocabulary is difficult to learn as English borrows from many languages, creating irregular spelling and pronunciation patterns. It also contains many words with similar meanings but subtle differences in usage. English also contains a lot of words. The Oxford English Dictionary defines about 600 000 words.
You can use this book to:

- Make a list of all the words you come across that you do not know. This will give you the best spelling list – words that you don't know but could come across at school or elsewhere.

- Review the list periodically.

- Cover the left hand side of each page and see if you can remember what the words are and put them in a sentence.

- Put a tick alongside the words that you become confident with and move on to the words that are not yet embedded in your vocabulary. However, return to these words in a few months for a final review.

- Use other resources such as Quizlet to help you become familiar with these words.

- Use write-cover-check to help you with words you find difficult to spell (page 79).

"The secret of getting ahead is getting started."
Samuel Clemens (Mark Twain), 1835 - 1910

Word	Definition

> "Words are the voice of the heart."
> Confucius (c. 551-c. 479 BC), Chinese philosopher

Word	Definition

"Hyperpolysyllabicomania is a fondness for big words."
unknown

Word	Definition

Congratulations, you have now learned 20 new words. Now is a good time to go back and revise. ☺

> "The more that you read, the more things you will know. The more that you learn, the more places you'll go."
> Dr. Seuss, 1904 – 1991

Word	Definition

> "The most important thing is to read as much as you can, like I did. It will give you an understanding of what makes good writing and it will enlarge your vocabulary."
> J.K. Rowling, 1965 -

Word	Definition

> *"One forgets words as one forgets names. One's vocabulary needs constant fertilizing or it will die."*
> *Evelyn Waugh, 1903 – 1966*

Word	Definition

Congratulations, you have now learned 40 new words. Now is a good time to go back and revise. ☺

> "Loving your language means a command of its vocabulary beyond the level of the everyday."
> John McWhorter, 1965 -

Word	Definition

> "Without trust, words become the hollow sound of a wooden gong. With trust, words become life itself."
> John Harold, 1873 - 1947

Word	Definition

> "Use the big thinker's vocabulary. Use big, bright, cheerful words. Use words that promise victory, hope, happiness, pleasure, avoid words that create unpleasant images of failure, defeat, grief."
> David. J. Schwartz, 1927 – 1987

Word	Definition

Congratulations, you have now learned 60 new words. Now is a good time to go back and revise. ☺

> "Words, once they're printed, have a life of their own."
> Carol Burnett, 1933 -

Word	Definition

"In every case, the remedy is to take action. Get clear about exactly what it is that you need to learn and exactly what you need to do to learn it."
Miguel de Cervantes, 1547-1616

Word	Definition

"*Live as if your were to die tomorrow. Learn as if you were to live forever.*"
Mohandas (Mahatma) Gandhi. 1869-1948

Word	Definition

Congratulations, you have now learned 80 new words.

> "A man with a scant vocabulary will almost certainly be a weak thinker. The richer and more copious one's vocabulary and the greater one's awareness of fine distinctions and subtle nuances of meaning, the more fertile and precise is likely to be one's thinking. Knowledge of things and knowledge of the words for them grow together. If you do not know the words, you can hardly know the thing."
> Henry Hazlitt, 1894 - 1993

Word	Definition

> *"Yes, you can be a dreamer and a doer too, if you will remove one word from your vocabulary: impossible."*
> Robert H. Schuller, 1926 -

Word	Definition

"Writers fish for the right words like fishermen fish for, um, whatever those aquatic creatures with fins and gills are called. "
Jarod Kintz, 1982 -

Word	Definition

Congratulations, you have now learned 100 new words. You have become a real wordsmith. ☺

> *"Will I have to use a dictionary to read your book?" asked Mrs. Dodypol. "It depends," says I, "how much you used the dictionary before you read it."*
> *Alexander Theroux, 1939 -*

| Word | Definition |
| --- | --- |ುದು

"Few activities are as delightful as learning new vocabulary."
Tim Gunn, 1953 -

Word	Definition

> *"For me, reading has always been not only a quest for pleasure and enlightenment but also a word-hunting expedition, a lexical safari."*
> *Charles Harrington Elster, 1957 -*

Word	Definition

Congratulations, you have now learned 120 new words.

> *"Right!" "Right!"*
> *"You can get there!" "I can get there!"*
> *"You're a natural at counting to two!"*
> *"I'm a nat'ral at counting to two!"*
> *"If you can count to two, you can count to anything!"*
> *"If I can count to two, I can count to anything!"*
> *"And then the world is your mollusc!"*
> *"My mollusc! What's a mollusc?"*
> *Terry Pratchett, 1948 - , Men at Arms: The Play*

Word	Definition

"Never use a big word when a diminutive will suffice."
Unknown

Word	Definition

> "By reading so much, my vocabulary automatically improved along with my comprehension."
> Ben Carson, 1951 -

Word	Definition

Congratulations, you have now learned 140 new words. Now is a good time to go back and revise. ☺

> "The limits of my language are the limits of my universe" (translated from the German)
> Johann Wolfgang von Goethe, 1749 - 1832

Word	Definition

"Any fool can know. The point is to understand."
Albert Einstein, 1879 - 1955

Word	Definition

> "The love of learning, the sequestered nooks,
> And all the sweet serenity of books"
> Henry Wadsworth Longfellow, 1807 - 1882

Word	Definition

Congratulations, you have now learned 160 new words.
Now is a good time to go back and revise. ☺

"The more you read, the more you know.
The more you know, the smarter you grow.
The smarter you grow, the stronger your voice,
when speaking your mind or making your choice."

| Word | Definition |
| --- | --- |****

> "The more I read, the more I acquire, the more certain I am that I know nothing."
> Voltaire, 1694 - 1778

Word	Definition

> *"Learning never exhausts the mind."*
> *Leonardo da Vinci, 1452 - 1519*

Word	Definition

Congratulations, you have now learned 180 new words.
Now is a good time to go back and revise. ☺

"Learning is not attained by chance, it must be sought for with ardor and attended to with diligence."
Abigail Adams, 1744 - 1818

Word	Definition

"Learning is a treasure that will follow its owner everywhere."
Chinese Proverb

Word	Definition

"The difference between a successful person and others is not a lack of strength, not a lack of knowledge, but rather a lack of will."
Vince Lombardi, 1913 - 1970

Word	Definition

Congratulations, you have now learned 200 new words. Well done on your perseverance, keep it up. ☺

"Every great dream begins with a dreamer. Always remember, you have within you the strength, the patience, and the passion to reach for the stars to change the world."
Harriet Tubman, 1822 - 1913

Word	Definition

> "When something seems difficult, dare to do it anyway."
> Steve Maraboli, 1975 -

Word	Definition

> "When the day has ended, dare to feel as you've done your best.
> Dare to be the best you can."
> Steve Maraboli, 1975 -

Word	Definition

Congratulations, you have now learned 220 new words. Now is a good time to go back and revise. ☺

> "What we hope ever to do with ease, we must learn first to do with diligence."
> Samuel Johnson, (1709-1784

Word	Definition

"Keep steadily before you the fact that all true success depends at last upon yourself."
Theodore T. Hunger

Word	Definition

"If we encounter a man of rare intellect, we should ask him what books he reads."
Ralph Waldo Emerson, 1803 - 1882

Word	Definition

Congratulations, you have now learned 240 new words. Now is a good time to go back and revise. ☺

"You know you've read a good book when you turn the last page and feel a little as if you have lost a friend."
Paul Sweeney

Word	Definition

"Aim for the moon. If you miss, you may hit a star."
W. Clement Stone, 1902 - 2002

Word	Definition

> *"Good things come to people who wait, but better things come to those who go out and get them."*
> *Anonymous*

Word	Definition

Congratulations, you have now learned 260 new words. Now is a good time to go back and revise. ☺

> *"I find that the harder I work, the more luck I seem to have."*
> Thomas Jefferson, 1743 - 1826

Word	Definition

> "Success is the sum of small efforts, repeated day-in and day-out."
> Robert Collier, 1885 - 1950

Word	Definition

> "So many books, so little time."
> Frank Zappa, 1940 - 1993

Word	Definition

Congratulations, you have now learned 280 new words. Now is a good time to go back and revise. ☺

"There is no friend as loyal as a book."
Ernest Hemingway, 1899 - 1961

Word	Definition

> "That's the thing about books. They let you travel without moving your feet."
> *Jhumpa Lahiri, 1967 -*

Word	Definition

"Success is dependent on effort."
Sophocles, c.496BC – 406BC

Word	Definition

Congratulations, you have now learned 300 new words. You have earned the title of novice lexicoligist. ☺

> *"I never feel lonely if I've got a book - they're like old friends. Even if you're not reading them over and over again, you know they are there."*
> *Emilia Fox, 1974 -*

| Word | Definition |
| --- | --- |ни

"Reading is to the mind what exercise is to the body."
Joseph Addison, 1671 - 1719

Word	Definition

"They succeed, because they think they can."
Virgil, 70BC – 19BC

Word	Definition

Congratulations, you have now learned 320 new words. Now is a good time to go back and revise. ☺

"Lucy: You learn more when you lose
Charlie Brown: Well then I must be the smartest person in world!!!"
Charles M. Schulz, 1922 – 2000, Peanuts Treasury

Word	Definition

> "The road to success is dotted with many tempting parking spaces."
> Will Rogers, 1879 - 1935

Word	Definition

> "The only place success comes before work is in the dictionary."
> Vince Lombardi, 1913 - 1970

Word	Definition

Congratulations, you have now learned 340 new words. Now is a good time to go back and revise. ☺

> *"Books are the quietest and most constant of friends; they are the most accessible and wisest of counselors, and the most patient of teachers."*
> Charles William Eliot, 1834 - 1926

Word	Definition

> "There is no elevator to success…you have to take the stairs."
> Zig Ziglar, 1926 - 2012

Word	Definition

> "Successful people read more books."
> Unknown

Word	Definition

Congratulations, you have now learned 360 new words. Now is a good time to go back and revise. ☺

> *"The etymologist finds the deadest words to have been once a brilliant picture. Language is fossil poetry."*
> *Ralph Waldo Emerson, , 1803 - 1882*

Word	Definition

> "This week I've been reading a lot and doing little work. That's the way things ought to be. That's surely the road to success."
> Anne Frank, 1929 - 1945

Word	Definition

"Be awesome! Be a book nut!"
Dr. Seuss, 1904 - 1991

Word	Definition

Congratulations, you have now learned 380 new words. Now is a good time to go back and revise. ☺

> "The way of success is the way of continuous pursuit of knowledge."
> Napoleon Hill, 1883 – 1970, Think and Grow Rich

| Word | Definition |

"No matter what people tell you, words and ideas can change the world."
Robin Williams, 1951 - 2014

Word	Definition

> "Read. Read. Read. Just don't read one type of book. Read different books by various authors so that you develop different styles."
> R. L. Stine, 1943 -

Word	Definition

Congratulations, you have now learned 400 new words. Amazing, stupendous, wonderful, astounding, phenomenal. ☺

"Today I am leading because yesterday I was reading."
Amit Kalantri, 1988 -

Word	Definition

> "Books are a staircase to unknown worlds."
> Jason Ellis, 1971 -

Word	Definition

> "To be able to speak and be able to have clarity and to be able to think. Those are the greatest of gifts."
> Bill Cosby, 1937 -

Word	Definition

Congratulations, you have now learned 420 new words. Now is a good time to go back and revise. ☺

> "Kind words do not cost much. Yet they accomplish much."
> Blaise Pascal, 1623 - 1662

Word	Definition

"My words fly up, my thoughts remain below; Words without thoughts never to heaven go."
William Shakespeare, 1564-1616

Word	Definition

> "One cannot guess how a word functions. One has to look at its use and learn from that."
> Ludwig Wittgenstein, 1889 - 1951

Word	Definition

Congratulations, you have now learned 440 new words. Now is a good time to go back and revise. ☺

"Never regard study as a duty, but as the enviable opportunity to learn to know the liberating influence of beauty in the realm of the spirit for your own personal joy and to the profit of the community to which your later work belongs."
Albert Einstein, 1879-1955

Word	Definition

> "I don't care how long it takes me, I'm going somewhere beautiful."
> Unknown

Word	Definition

"If you deliberately plan on being less than you are capable of being, then I warn you that you'll be unhappy for the rest of your life."
Abraham Maslow, 1908 - 1970

Word	Definition

Congratulations, you have now learned 460 new words.
Now is a good time to go back and revise. ☺

> *I am thankful to all those who said NO to me,*
> *It's because of them I did it myself.*
> *Albert Einstein, 1879-1955*

Word	Definition

> "I'm not telling you it's going to be easy - I'm telling you it's going to be worth it."
> Arthur (Art) Williams, 1942 -

Word	Definition

"The reading of all good books is like conversation with the finest men of the past centuries."
René Descartes, 1596 - 1650

Word	Definition

Congratulations, you have now learned 480 new words. Now is a good time to go back and revise. ☺

> "Always do your best. What you plant now, you will harvest later."
> Og Mandino, 1923 - 1996

Word	Definition

> "Success is the result of perfection, hard work, learning from failure, loyalty, and persistence."
> Colin Powell, 1937 -

Word	Definition

Before anything else, preparation is the key to success.
Alexander Graham Bell, 1847 - 1922

Word	Definition

**Congratulations, you have now learned 500 new words.
You have now earned the title of lexicologist.
Great work.** ☺
Remember to revise or you will forget some.

> "Ambition is the path to success. Persistence is the vehicle you arrive in."
> Bill Bradley, 1943 -

Write – Cover – Check

For any words that you find difficult to spell, write – cover – check, remains a valuable method to help. Carefully copy the word into the first column, then cover before writing in the second. Later, try writing again in the third column

Write	Cover	Check

Write	Cover	Check

Write	Cover	Check

Write	Cover	Check

Write	Cover	Check

Write	Cover	Check

Write	Cover	Check

Write	Cover	Check

Write	Cover	Check
___	___	___
___	___	___
___	___	___
___	___	___
___	___	___
___	___	___
___	___	___
___	___	___
___	___	___
___	___	___
___	___	___
___	___	___
___	___	___
___	___	___
___	___	___
___	___	___
___	___	___
___	___	___
___	___	___
___	___	___
___	___	___
___	___	___
___	___	___

Write	Cover	Check

Write	Cover	Check

Write	Cover	Check

Write	Cover	Check

Write	Cover	Check

Write	Cover	Check

Write	Cover	Check

Write	Cover	Check

Write	Cover	Check

Write	Cover	Check

Write	Cover	Check

Write	Cover	Check

Write	Cover	Check

Write	Cover	Check

Write	Cover	Check

Write	Cover	Check

Write	Cover	Check

Write	Cover	Check

Write	Cover	Check

A list of words which are difficult to spell.

Here is a list of frequently misspelled words. Why not have a look and see if there are any that you can't spell? Why not ask an adult to read them out and see if you can write them down correctly?

abundant	column
acceptable	committee
accidently	conclusion
accommodate	cough
ache	daughter
acquire	deciduous
across	definitely
acrylic	dilemma
ancient	disappointed
audience	ecstasy
bizarre	eerie
bought	embarrassed
cemetery	enough
colleague	exceed

existence	height
existence	height
extension	hierarchy
familiar	humorous
fierce	ignorance
fiery	immediately
foreign	independent
foreseeable	intelligent
forty	interrupt
fourth	knowledge
friend	library
gauge	licence
gist	loathe
glamorous	lovely
government	maintain
graffiti	maintenance
guarantee	miniature
happened	necessary
harass	nervous

noticeable	sieve
obey	supersede
occasion	truly
papyrus	twelfth
pastime	unforeseen
permanent	until
possession	wherever
preferred	
preparation	
proceed	
pronunciation	
publicly	
questionnaire	
receive	
relevant	
research	
rhythm	
schedule	
separate	

A list of challenging words.

Here is a list of very challenging words. Quite a few of these words have two or more meanings. Why not have a look through the list and any you are unsure of, look up and add to the main part of this book?

abode

abundance

alert

altitude

ample

antiquity

apprehensive

beck

benefit

bewildered

chaos

clemency

complex

conceited

conclusion

content

contract

covet

coy

debrief

deliberate

demolished

derelict

device

din

dismal

drought

emerge

evaluation	orthodontist
extinction	passive
families	peak
flamboyant	perplexed
foe	physiotherapy
frivolous	pigment
gregarious	polarity
helix	pompous
humble	precarious
inaugurate	resort
incision	rigid
inconspicuous	shrink
inferior	slope
inhabitants	subdued
intense	submissive
isolation	subterfuge
length	subterranean
nauseous	succumb
nurseryman	summit

superfluous

teenager

tempestuous

traders

tranquil

trivia

trivial

uniform

unorthodox

unsurpassed

vanished

vicarious

volatile

volcano

wound

www.ingramcontent.com/pod-product-compliance
Lightning Source LLC
Chambersburg PA
CBHW072101110526
44590CB00018B/3269